Order this book online at www.trafford.com
or email orders@trafford.com

Most Trafford titles are also available at major online book retailers.

Print information available on the last page.

ISBN: 978-1-4669-7080-9 (sc)
ISBN: 978-1-4669-7079-3 (hc)
ISBN: 978-1-4907-6470-2 (e)

Library of Congress Control Number: 2012922764

Trafford rev. 08/31/2015

 www.trafford.com

North America & international
toll-free: 1 888 232 4444 (USA & Canada)
fax: 812 355 4082

Out

of the

Earth

An Imperative Anthology
By
Butch Houchens

Out of the Earth I grew
With a soiled face and
Tattered shoe.

And still her adornments
I do wear in faded jeans
And graying hair.

Acknowledgments

From an early age, my feet were wet and my face soiled from my immersion into the natural world. So, I would like to thank my parents for allowing me to get dirty and play in the creek. I owe much of what I am and know about the earth to that freedom and I strongly advocate that every child should have as much access and exposure to the workings of nature as possible. I would like to not only thank my mother for allowing me to bring home and keep every kind of critter imaginable, but also to apologize to her for the snakes that escaped into my room and startled her many times. I owe a special thanks to my father, who from the very beginning, never left the house to fish or hunt without his son in company. I learned to love the Earth simply from my contact with it, he taught me to respect it and how to use it! My father didn't take me to exotic places because we lived a very modest life. Rather, we roamed the Ragged Mountains of central Virginia and waded the nearby rivers and streams. So, that's where this book will take you, not to Everest but to Bear Den Mountain, not to the Amazon but to Biscuit Run Creek. Without the freedom to intimately experience the elements, the Earth, and it's amazing life, none of this would have been possible.

My parents also took me to church where my concept of the human spirit began. My knowledge of the life of Jesus Christ has been a stabilizing and inspiring influence and I have drawn guidance from his example and teachings almost daily over the years.

I would also like to acknowledge Caroline Polk/Swope, of Polk Editorial Services, who proof read my work and helped me make it presentable, Matthew Davidson for his layout and graphics assistance, and Don Hirsch, who, in his always gracious manner, read through the poetry and gave me just the right feedback at just the right time.

And last, but certainly not least, I would like to acknowledge the significant and lasting impact of my Mother-in-law, Barbara Reynolds, who through her tireless and often heroic efforts at Lake Reynovia, made outdoor recreation available not only to me but also to countless thousands of others.

Table of Contents

Section I

Introduction

The purpose of my life and, consequently of this book, is to celebrate and now, in some cases, lament man's enduring relationship with the place of his generation and habitation the Earth! My desire has always been to awaken or call to memory in ourselves something deeper and longer lasting than our transient affairs with entertainment, economics, fashion, and technology all of which are fickle and fleeting at best. I believe that our devotion, (and when I say devotion I'm referring to actions), should be to earthly matters; family, fellowship, natural living, sharing, simplicity, self -restraint, romance, peace, sustainable systems, self-reliance and laughter, to mention just a few.

It is my fear that if we, for much longer, view our time upon the Earth as a sprint of exploitation and domination rather than as a marathon of co-existence and endurance, we as a species, will cross the finish line far ahead of schedule. Make no mistake, our days upon the Earth are numbered by forces beyond our control! But in the interim, how large that number becomes, for the most part, will depend on how we choose to interact with the

Earth and the ecosystems that have developed within the thin ribbon of life on its surface.

On our present, unaltered course, we will continue to discover that we have traded the abundant "riches" of our waters and land and their life-sustaining ability for mountains of discarded "necessities" and waters laden with the by-products to produce them. In fact, this is already a stark reality in many quarters of the natural world and because of related human activity like over harvesting and habitat loss, many species are struggling to survive. Unfortunately, there are many people who have little awareness of how their activities as a consumer and their initiatives toward economic excesses have adversely affected our environment. Such seemingly benign acts, as introducing non-native plants into the home landscape, are drastically and permanently changing the composition of soils, the types of trees and plants that are growing in our forests, and subjecting important native species to the devastating effects of exposure to pests against which they have no defenses. Today, literally hundreds of exotic plant and animal species introduced into this country are either gaining a foot hold or causing the decline or demise of important native species.

From the experiences in my own life, I have no doubt that it will be the natural laws, which govern the Earth and all the forces therein, that will determine our fate, not the strength of the economy or the range of our missiles into outer space.

Optimally, our heritage should be an intact, flourishing and sustainable natural world and children with at least some knowledge of its workings. Further, our life styles should be more in harmony with and have a less severe impact on the things which are most critical to our long term well-being on the earth; specifically water resources, food production, bio diversity, air quality, and weather systems to mention a few.

For those of you who view a life living within the boundaries of natural laws as a sacrifice, it is quite the contrary. It's enlightenment! . . the likes of which most of us will never see. Adherence to those laws allows others who live here with us (the animals) to navigate without instruments, see without eyes, and know without government or counsel! In my mind, the greatest frontiers yet to be explored are the innate abilities of man and the human spirit that guides our actions. As for me, my head is in the clouds, whenever they descend to five feet, eight inches; my feet and hopes planted in the moist, rich, living soil and waters of the Earth, not the dry, desolate, dead, dust of the moon or beyond!

It is my hope, through sharing this collection of poetry, that you may see the earth as I do, simply beautiful and come to love some piece of it or thing upon it, thereby *causing you to want to experience the earth as I have and then protect and preserve it for others (like our children) to witness and enjoy.*

For many of you, these poems will simply remind you of what you already know, that the Earth is inspiration and delight; sensitive but resilient; amazingly powerful, even dangerous, yet accessible. I hope you enjoy getting your feet wet!

Fragments of script in time,
Too short for eloquence,
Too rushed for rhyme.
I know life's the same,
And it makes no sense,
I can't long be what I became!

Author hiking in the Blue Ridge, 1970

BUTCH HOUCHENS

Section I

A Place For Us

Try to color life as brilliant
As Indian Paint Brush and Flax
So that the winds of time
Find it difficult to erase your tracks.

Man of Toil

I am not a man of letters
Or a poet entranced, you see.
I'm the man of toil and a sweater,
The very grit of humanity.
I lived not on Walden
And wore no lace upon my shirt.
There was neither dowry, or stipend
Nor mansion for me to desert.
Yet, I ascended Ben Bulben's
Majestic head and stood
For a moment on the lake,
A noble visitor instead.

Keswick Sunset

The evening unfolded her hands to me
As softly as the opening of a flower
And displayed her wondrous sights
In the day's last waning hour.

As dark clouds capped with
Cream slowly rumbled by
And flocks of honking geese
Descended from the ever
Darkening sky,

I stood before my God
And uttered a simple little
Prayer of thanks for His
Majesty upon the Earth
And my presence there.

Cataloochee

There's new light in the Cataloochee shadows
For majestic bull elk bugle there again!
No longer silent are Smoky Mountain meadows
Where he tends the harem with a musk stained chin.

Too long, it's been, since we last saw morning
Mists off the wildly rushing stream
Rise up the dew glistening valley before joining
The hot breaths spewing puffs of steam.

There have been no tracks, rubs or wallows
Since that last, fatal musket shot
And no rut to thrill the hills & hollows
Where cows and calves now, hardily trot.

Count me as among the most fortunate
To witness this renewed, wild, natural scene
As I exhort you all, my brothers, do not forget
To keep what's left of Mother Nature, pristine!

Mountain Meadow

In the wild, blueberry meadow,
I lay down before my feast
And tracked the summer sun
As it moved west, from east.
I filled my heart with that sunshine
And free mountain air
Then rose to forage with the towhee
And lumbering black bear.
Come gently, now, old sow,
I'll bow to your fluffy little cubs
Then, I'll pick beneath the crags
And settle by the gooseberry shrubs.
Hum-bumble bees, flutter-by butterflies,
To find a nourishing flower
As I wonder how many insects
The swallows eat each hour.

Gently, sweetly, winds rustle by
Caressing my waiting, uplifted face
And creating images of dancing flowers
My mind could never erase.
Milkweed heads also sway lightly,
Releasing their heavenly smell.
The aroma followed me down the deer path
And we settled in the dell.
There, amid ripe blackberries,
Gold finch wings and unknown things to see
I cleansed my mind with nature, so kind.
In the mountain meadow, I'm free!
Then, at the end, before my fading eyes
See even the faintest shadow
Please, raise my spirit again, Lord
And carry me back to the meadow!

Trees

From where I sat, bundled and warm
On the sun dappled and wind swept hill,
The exposed trees seemed to shiver
In the late day's blustery chill.
Their lush, green canopy of summer
Is now a full-moon cycle off in the past
And their splendid colors of autumn
Are a show no longer being cast.
The tough, dry leaves that remain
Are drab olive or crisp earthen brown
But soon, they too, will join their loose-stemmed
Brothers being scattered across the ground.
Through the winter, each will stand there
Reduced to cold, bare skin and bones
But I will still recognize my resting friends,
By their unique form and lovely, gray wood tones.
And when the ice-days are finally broken
So, winter no longer dominates the frozen hills,
I'll celebrate as each sleeping tree is awoken
To participate in the spring's new living thrills!

The Little Stream

Wanting solitude in a stream's refreshments
On the 50th anniversary of my coming to Earth,
I shed all the trappings and vestments
Not present at the hour of my birth.

There, I reclined, until late into the sixth hour
Fully knowing what I had come to seek
Strength from its un-proclaimed power
And renewal in the waters of the little creek.

Alone, some would say I sat in the pool,
Insulated from the sun's searing heat.
While it took from June everything usually cool,
Crayfish foraged comfortably at my feet.

I acknowledged the tree's sheltering presence,
Watched minnows investigate the wilds of my skin
And opened my heart to accept the presents
Tranquilly bestowed by the rest of my kin.

And to this day, I cannot measure
Or even begin to fully comprehend
The depth and worth of the treasure
I received before that day's dreaded end.

So, as I fondly recall once again,
Those hours I spent naked in the stream,
I'm glad it's somewhere I've been
And not just something I dreamed.

Peacock Feathers and Powder

There's nothing left of me but
Peacock feathers and powder!
Please, pass me my slippers and
Could you speak a little louder!

Gone are the days of 'wild man'
I'm moving toward sedentary.
Now, from my balcony I scan,
The life I pursued in a hurry!

Don't count me out quite yet.
I'm only here in the evening.
My mornings are fraught with sweat
From my body's daily heaving.

It's my spare time, my joy
I have had to sacrifice.
I still work all day Old' boy!
At night, I pack on the ice.

Gingerly, I prop up my feet,
Or the prone position I take
Then from the discomfort of my seat,
I recall my days at the lake.

My bow and arrows are sheathed
And back pack semi-retired
I would have never believed
That I could be this uninspired.

I suppose that three score years
Is not a lot to be
So, with my debt in the arrears,
I toil on, endlessly.

The hammer and shovel I wield
Each day till the job is done
But my mind is always afield;
My heart longing for some fun.

I still have life left in me,
Dreams a-plenty and desire.
What I lack is enough energy
To work and then, Stoke the Fire!

Campfire

Sitting 'round the campfire's amber glow,
Heels snug against the smooth stones
To warm both heart and tingling toes
And foil the cold's attack on the bones.
It's warm flickering light does cast
Peace on the circle of smiling faces,
Spreading it equally upon the first and last
To come and claim their favorite places.
Long into the night the embers crackle
As sparks dance skyward on the heat
Illuminating every little laugh and cackle
Rising on the voice of contentment, so sweet.

Children

If upon the winds of time you flew
And every thought of mans' heart you knew.
　　How far away the world would be . . . .
Beyond sight and the grasp of me.
　　If you knew from where the clouds came
Or called all things by their proper name,
　　Tell me, what good would it be
Without warmth, love and family.
　　So what, if I work to save the trees
Or plow my fields and keep honey bees . . . .
　　If my children I don't love and know
And my gentle kindness I never show.
　　Oh, people say that the end is near,
That earthquakes and war we should fear;
　　And so possibly it's true,
But the greater loss or gain is within you.
　　For God measures not only by time
But also by quality in the family line.
　　So, if you pass on the scars of your strife,
A worse place has come to life.

The Vigilant Gardener

Darn you daisy fleabane!
Your delicate white flowers
Always temper my disdain
For the weeds along my garden path.
And though, I spend hours
Pulling all the rest;
Well, maybe not all
As I think and laugh,
For the evening primrose stands tall
With its sleek amber towers
And the may weeds gold buttons
Often put my heart to the test.

Distracted

Many a morning, I sat secluded and waiting
Constantly scanning, anxiously anticipating
The arrival of my wild, table fare
Only to find myself completely entranced,
My hunting day and life richly enhanced
By the creatures that abide out there.

On this cold, overcast and blustery day,
I watched three young otters catch fish and play
In the Edgerton's little valley pond
And gazed at flocks of songbirds filling the sky
As they dipped and swerved attempting to fly
South ahead of the snows in the mountains and
beyond.

Oak Hill

On an ancient ridge in old Virginia,
Stands the stately brick house at Oak Hill,
Where the gray mists of cool fall mornings
Settle gracefully on the valley's little rill.

Its long, grassy lawns lay open
As a gesture of far reaching hospitalities
And likewise, standing tall in their midst
Are the two hundred year old oak trees!

While iced tea is served on the verandah,
And everyone breaks from their chores,
Deer browse on the crop of fallen acorns
And squirrels peer from old woodpecker bores.

As the retrievers leave the glowing hearth
For their daily walk to the edge of the lawns,
The raccoon retreats to its den aloft
And the doe alerts her yearlings and fawns.

But no one retreats to leave completely.
They merely move obligingly to the side.
So, that those who dwell in the house and
Among the trees, together, peacefully abide.

But, when the afternoon sun casts long
Shadows behind everything standing erect,
There appears from the forests to the south
More creatures than any one would expect,

The little red fox trots the faint paths on
Hunting trips to and from his earthen den
And the coyote sniffs every track and
Trail where the cottontail rabbit has been.

Then, once in a great while, when no one
Expects to ever see them there,
There appears on a secluded edge or corner
The bobcat, a black panther or a bear.

So, the stately brick house and lawns
Of Oak Hill are only half of this story;
It's the creatures that share its wilds
That complete its earthly glory.

Excuse Me!

There were no others present
In the garden but me and him;
The tiny, black-capped chick-a-Dee
Perched on a shady limb.
I know his mate has eggs in my
Mail box post where she's nesting,
So, I thought I startled him
While he sat nearby, resting.
Because he looked at me,
As though slightly ill-at-ease,
I withdrew a step or two
From under the Crepe Myrtle trees.

To my surprise, he immediately
Flew in my direction!
He was not startled at all
I decided under close inspection.
Rather, he was on a bee-line
Straight to the bird bath.
He was waiting for me to leave;
I was blocking his path!
So, I withdrew further to the
Stone slabs of my garden seat
And waited there for the next
Adventure in my garden retreat.

Selu is the primary spiritual Deity of the Cherokee Indians. She is the keeper of all things living and growing on the earth. She is closely associated with the harvests, fertility and the rebirth of spring . . . .

Cherokee Deity

*On a quiet, still evening in May
I, in awe, did briefly stand
On a once nameless tract of
Now Selu Conservancy land.*

*It lay gracefully, at a point
Where a timid spring-let arose
And quickly intersected the meandering
Little River's near motionless flows.*

*I weaved my way through the twisted
And gnarled swamp willow trees
That stood stooped in tall emerald
Green grass up to their scruffy knees.*

*I expected a soggy bottom of silt and
Brown water oozing up around my feet
But encountered instead an elevated
Pathway through the wetland retreat.*

OUT OF THE EARTH

The farther I penetrated the miniature
Delta's diverse and colorful wilderness,
The harder my heart pulled me to tarry
And absorb a spiritual place such as this!

There was not a view devoid of clusters
Of wild Iris blades sprouting anew
Or bright yellow butter cup heads above
The vegetation they were poking up through.

And standing among them, some towering
Unreachable above the flowers and weeds,
Were shaggy tufts, like gnarly-wooled sheep
Grazing atop old, dried cattail reeds.

At a place where the marshes loam turned
To silted sand and dove under the water's seal,
There lay empty clam shells and fish scale
Clumps from an otter's recent aquatic meal.

Nearby, pressed deeply into the slowly drying
Mud were lines of three toed impressions,
Like fossil dinosaur tracks, from the stealthy
Great blue heron's stilt-legged processions.

Theirs was not the only evidence
Of creatures entering great and small;
There were bird nests and beaver gnaws
With splayed deer tracks traversing it all.

I greatly desired a specimen, a slip of
Watercress or Iris, to take home with me
But quickly replanted it in the mire, not
Wanting to disturb the simple complexity.

I had already left too many tracks
And gently pushed a few things aside.
Ultimately, I took only spirit from the place
And left all the others to peacefully abide.

So, I opened my newly elevated heart
And gave thanks for Selu's presentation,
Praying that those forming her future chart
Would always consider her preservation.

At Midnight

High above the village
On a knoll's wooded crown,
The "hoot-hoo" of an owl
Pierces the night's silent sound.
While I listen and ponder wood smoke
Mingled with cool mountain air,
I wonder who, if anyone is doing
The same in the valley down there?
Am I the only one listening
To the owl tonight
While gazing at the stars' soft,
Twinkling light?
How can the other young men sleep,
The night quietly passing them by?
Oh! I remember, they're tired and resting.
Sadly, so now, must I.

Ocracoke

The tent is pitched just one tall dune
Away from the ocean's surf on the beach.
Where its constant crash and roar remind
Me of what's within my easy reach.

Sea Oat blades, perfect for dancing
With the wind's often repeating touch,
Etch the hot, white-sand paths with the
Skill of an artist-directed brush.

Black tufts of sun-dried, sea grass lie
In broken lines at the crest of the beach
As hordes of scurrying sand fleas ride
The tide line to stay just out of reach.

Piles of orange, shell-shards, sorted and
Laid to rest by the surf's crashing waves
Are just another of the wildly dancing
Ocean's many multi-colored slaves.

But I'll not tell you another word of it,
Lest you not come and see it for yourself,
For these images cannot be aptly told
By me or all the sea books on the shelf.

Waterfront Cafe'

Dockside umbrellas of turquoise and azure
Flap fancifully before the island winds of June
As Pelicans preen primordial feathers, and the
Tall masts and spar lines whistle and rattle in tune.

Sun and water exact a daily toll on the posts
And boards of cedar, cypress and southern pine
Fading all but the metal roof tops to gray and
Green along shimmering, Silver Lake's shore line.

A rugged, yet tranquil place where pirate history,
Mariners and tourists interplay to the sublime,
While the ferry ride to the mainland keeps in check
The outside's reckless race through time.

The Unguided Tour?

Tell little elvers, how do you,
So accurately, navigate?
Parents having succumbed
To Sargasso's grizzly fate!
They all lie dead on the bottom
Of the great calm sea;
Nothing left but eggs
And your long, incredible journey.
Upon hatching, every tiny,
Clear European eel sliver
Turn east, while the young Americans
Swim for a western river.
Escaping all the dangers
In the vast ocean's rolling swell,
They ascend every drainage,
Seeking a place to dwell,
There residing seven years
Before being mysteriously drawn
Back to the Sargasso Sea
To repeat the wiggling spawn.

Chesapeake

When Michener described scenes of its fading glory,
I took it to be little more than an embellished story
Of historic man, innumerable crabs and exploited birds.
But discovered the essence of those many, true words,
When under the spell of endless, natural pleasure,
I, too, joined the harvest of its awesome treasure.
And thought naught, of my limited presence there,
Beyond my quarry, its capture and days being fair.
I could not see beyond its rippled waters glistening
Or comprehend the warnings in spite of my listening
To reports of decline and demise, amid forecasts so bleak,
For the mighty, fragile waters of the great Chesapeake!

When I look out across its broad, meandering expanse,
My eyes dismiss the concept there could ever be a chance
That this vast nursery of creatures great and small
Might be teetering on the brink of collapse for them all.
And then, I realized that "them all" also includes me;
That this estuary has now and throughout its history
Fed the native Americans and whoever went before
Then, sustained my ancestors who settled on its shore.
So, from this heritage, there are many entrenched voices
Who staunchly defend their access to the dwindling resources.
Whether from marshy shore or to the inland tributary creek,
Everyone wants their part, to the last piece of the Chesapeake.

Then, in one week, I saw four sea turtles rankly floating
And gagged at the stench of croakers grossly bloating
In tide lines atop the water's wind-driven swells
And gasped aloud, not at the thick, rotting fish smells,
But at the tons of tiny, dead, by-catch culls floating
'Round the net-fishermen's faded, red boat hulls.

It seemed, that in every quarter, death was the norm;
That in the old order of life brewed a building storm.
Blown in by the rampant development to the water's edge.
Yea, and by the heavy weight of the winter watermen's dredge.
But, of these things I was sorely afraid to loudly speak,
Lest I offend some user of the waters of the dying Chesapeake.

With every new report, my ears cringe all the more.
Hearing distress calls from distant drainage to adjacent shore .
Toxic chemicals are spreading both windward and lee
As the lands, bitter runoff moves deadly through to the sea
There now exists an enormous, mid-bay dead-zone
Where nothing abides or survives, save the water alone . . .
And, if this weren't enough, there arose out of Greedville
Fleets of boats and planes that take its life at their will
Depleting the once bountiful shoals so much each day
That vast stocks of resources have slowly dwindled away.
But, it's not unusual for men, their earthly fortune to seek,
From the long chain of life, now broken in the Chesapeake.

Now, the alarm has sounded, let every man heed the bell.
Let no one be confounded or doubt the urgency of the knell
Calling us shoulder to shoulder, an about-face we must take
To limit the harvest and pollution, promising to not forsake
The lady of our sustenance from marshy creek to open bay
Pledging our commitment to its life, starting from this day.
Let those, who plant the lawns and them, who use the fields,
Know the choice is life in the bay or nitrogen from the yields.
Let no man surmise, that his piece not be the critical one
For the call needs to resound, from them who farm, trawl or gun
To those who trim the full, taught sails of sloops so sleek,
To forever protect the life sustaining waters of the Chesapeake

Room With A View

My worry about heaven
Is that I'll have a view of Earth
To helplessly see what I could have done,
Unable to walk its height or girth;
All my battles bequeathed to others, un-won.

So, I find it quite impossible
To long for some heavenly trip
And save my own worthless hide,
When our lives here we need to equip;
It's on the Earth I want to us abide.

Mocking Birds

I once stopped, while trekking on my way,
To watch two mocking birds in a mid-road fray.
Face to face they hopped but not a feather flew
And what they determined, only they knew.
For at the end, each did fly without peck or push
To opposite sides of the road and a berry-laden bush.
As fate would have it, nearly eight years to the day,
I, again, encountered a mid-road mocking bird fray.
There, face to face, they stood, confirming my suspicions
It's a ritual of territory!, Not a meeting of random conditions.
So, with delight, I watched them hop and flex their wings
Realizing, I know very little about them and other things.

Natural High

My desire is to ride the heavens like a cloud
Without first wearing that morbid shroud
Or sit atop fluttering woodcock wings
To fly high above the meadow as he sings.
Then cling like a bee to cherry blossom ends
As they dance on fragrant spring winds.

I could also watch the trees grow for a season
Without disruption, explanation or reason
Then curl up, cozy, in the leaves at one's trunk
Without thoughts of a house or made up bunk.
And gaze unceasingly at the clear, star-lit sky
Without any other light to clutter my eye.

He's mad", you say, "a hopeless romantic at best!
No realist would think to make such odd requests."
But, without Nature I could not endure life's pain
I absorb its harmony to keep me relatively sane!
And the internal peace, she's so free to impart
Is the natural drug that elevates my heart.

Monarch

Oh, Monarch, you are more than a mere butterfly,
For, God's Will upon the earth, you faithfully glorify!
In four generations, you fly north with the summer days
Then, turn south and winter in the Sierra Madres.
If only one of you accomplished this awesome migration,
It would still be a feat beyond my wildest imagination.
But, the heading is the same for each and every one
Whether started in the Dakotas or New England's autumn sun.
So, in your perfect heeding of nature's primal call,
You inspire the 'mighty' and set the example for us all.

Little Things

A single Geranium stem is blooming
Upon my window sill.
Its pink flowers warm in spite
Of winter's ice/white chill.
Alone and silent, not a word
Or clamor does it make
But still, into my heart, its simple
Messages I eagerly take;
A moment of comfort and hope
For better days on the way,
A bit of color in my life,
Something bright for the day . . .
And, if I could command all
Things, according to my will,
Everyone would be as kind as the
Little stem on my window sill.

The Woodcock

Into lofty heights the woodcock soars
To sing his melodious song as he swoops
And glides to the earth he so adores.
In every corner of the field he sits
Croaking in the same deep voice
Until ready for flight again he gets.
He starts at dusk on a spring moonlit night
Courting, mating, nesting, fill the hours
And inspire the flutter of each flight.
Now, if you should hear one, listen long
Because for going up and coming down
He has a completely different song.
So when in grassy pastures of spring you stand
Be glad . . . lift up your heart . . . . and listen
For this is woodcock land.

A Place To Enjoy

I had an afternoon free
That I wanted to enjoy,
    So, I drove back to the place
Where I had lived as a boy.
    Expecting to see things the same
And life still good,
    I was astonished to find it all changed;
Not a tree still stood.
    The valley where the creek forked
And I knew every bend
    Was now a wide flat place;
Miller's field was buried end-to-end.
    A pond used to be there
And a creek so full of life.
    Frogs, snakes, minnows and turtles;
All the things that know no strife.
    How could this be, that the little stream
Which had refreshed us all
    Was now gone; the reeds, the cattails,
Even bobwhite's call.
    As I stood there surveying
Where my bare little feet used to roam,
    I began to study the ground
that the people of the project call home.
    There's nothing here to learn,
No bees to watch, no creek to see,
    No fish to catch, or banks to jump
At the place where I ran free.

So, in this once peaceful place
I sat and thought of yester-year;
        Of sunny days, strawberries
And queen snakes, oh, how life was dear.
        Every now and again
A sweet contentment rolled over my soul,
        As I remembered my youth
And realized that I am not yet old.
        So, this one thing I began to wish
For every young adventurous girl and boy,
        That you may have the time
And a wild place to enjoy.

Shenandoah National Park, 2009

This poem was written while sitting on a steep ridge on the side of a mountain. It was late afternoon, and the towering, near leafless Tulip Poplar trees were rocking wildly as the winter wind roared down the mountain side.

Wind

The wind has no occasion for whining.
Yea, nor any form for defining
Its movement through time and space.
Save that it passes close to something else,
We are able to hear its frightful roar
Or see its dusty face!

Companions

My companions, the birds, say nothing I can understand.
They render me no service or wait for my command.
Rather, they summons me before the morning sky is lit
And require that I rise from my slumber
To cheerfully greet the day and its wonder,
Dreading not the rising but the coming hour of my respite.

. . . "wherefore your Creator loveth you much,
Seeing that He hath bestowed on you so many benefits."
Saint Francis of Assisi, on birds, 1220. ad.

Autumn

I broke through the majestic fortress
Of trunks and limbs loosely entwined
And succumbed to the colorful forces
That herald Summer's end, so defined.

Streams of filtered sunlight flickered
On long, bowing, golden-leafed fronds
As flocks of traveling birds bickered
To work out Nature's competitive bonds.

Dogwoods and maples, seemingly ablaze
In their magenta and cardinal splendor,
Were brilliantly framed by the yellow maze
The poplars and hickories chose to render.

The magnificence is not theirs to retain
In reserve for a refrain on the morrow
But to display, so briefly, without restraint
Lest, all re-enter winter in drab sorrow.

So, I wandered the painted valley in awe
Of autumn's amber and crimson bliss
And picked the last, sweet Pawpaw.
I never beheld a spectacle such as this!

For, gold and orange leaves of sassafras
Showed brightly 'round the forest's ruffled hem
And the stately, black gum boldly cast
A crown of royal, vermilion gems.

And, if one favor more I could glean,
Before receiving Nature's final kiss,
It would be that I could live so green
And die as colorful as this!

Section II

Out of the Heart

Introduction

The heart is nothing if not receptive. Its openness is the basis of our relationships and the gateway through which all human transactions must pass. It allows or denies beginnings, regulates the present, and has a perception of how it anticipates the future should play out. The well-being of the heart or human spirit, is one of the greatest responsibilities we have to ourselves and to our fellow man.

More beautiful than the flowers of the field
Are the gifts from your heart
And greater than the bountiful yield
Are the joys that you impart.

Blessed

If I were ever forced to choose and favor only one;
Then, it's you! You who loved me, for it is from that
Security that all my battles were won. I thought
Myself blessed to have parental love, then my siblings
Loved me too. I took a wife and found all the more,
And then my children's love I knew. How can I
Explain the strength I obtained when my friends
And others proclaimed, we also love you!
This book is not the result of a single love
Or two but the great and small love of you all that
Was mine my whole life through. A poet, I have
Always wanted to be, Thank you for the love
That allowed me to explore this liberty.

When the drought doeth come
And the tender grasses all wither
Causing some to eventually die,
Remember, the noblest of them all
Are the shoots that grow anew, knowing
They again must look death in the eye.

In My Heart

In my heart a volume of
Verse is stored,
     A living, yet dying, tribute
To the woman I adored.
     I would open it up
For everyone to see
     But, it's kept there in secret
Just to comfort me.

     Now, the poet I've become.
The walking remains
     Of some Love to great
To bear its loss.
     So, like Emily, I toss
These words inconsolably to the pen,
     That I like she,
Might scrawl some peace within.

So gracious am I in my solitude
The perfect host when I'm the only guest!
Of what value is my saintly attitude
If no one ever sees me at my best?

My Desire

I want to write
The loveliest poem there has ever been;
One with tenderness
And warmth subtly tucked within.
It would be filled with
Breathless sighs and butterflies.
Its lines of rhyme,
Would for me, have no end.

It would speak fondly
If eyes that long to gaze upon blue,
Contain an embrace of love,
A passionate kiss or two.
But as these lines
Materialize, I realize,
This poem is simply
My desire for more of you.

Currituck

Were you ever told, that once
Upon this windswept shore,
There lived an attendant
To everyone's sick door?
Though, he loved these water's
Near incessant wind on his face,
He never hesitated to leave for
Need at some near or distant place.
So, if you should visit and find these
Waters clear, reflective and calm,
They, too, are remembering the life, of
The sweet physician, William H. Romm.

Summer Love

Oh! How summer begins, fresh after spring,
 When all things are so new!
There's time for love and idle talk about life
 From a non-encompassing view.
No thoughts of yesterday or tomorrow;
 Summer is urgent for today.
Because once it's over, the incontestable
 Chill of fall is surely under way.
But, summer is past for me, unlike summer
 Has passed for you.
For I, in my deepest passion, cannot
 My summer renew . . .

Friendship

Thru thick and thin yesterday,
Today and life throughout,
Loyalty, love and support are
What friendships are all about.
Though sunny days and adventures,
Like the river, slowly, amble by,
The bonds of our friendships remain,
Time and distance they defy.

Your Love

Your laugh has made sweeter
And your touch made warmer
The most fragrant summer air.

And all who gather about you are
Showered with blessings, like cherry
Blossoms falling around a tree, so fair.

No one has stood closer to the tree than I,
Or looked up through those out-stretched
Branches white against the sea blue sky.

So, as I leave, drug sobbing away, I will
Always remember the beautiful tree
I saw blooming in the garden that day.

Lost Love

When I touch the petals
Of the softest little flowers
    Or recount the moments
Of my life's finest hours,
    Your face, so radiant,
Comes plainly into view.
    'Twas sweet love, not the passion,
That bound me to you.
    So, every sun that rises
To pass through the sullen air,
    May dry the morning dew
But not my tears of despair.

Where I am

In winter, when the sun
Warms the dried summer grasses
And a gentle breeze of peace
Over the meadow passes,
You can find me lying in
Raptured solitude there,
Cleansing my mind of worry,
Distress, and worldly care.

Wedding at Poplar Hill

I will meet you there, my Love
Where the splendid Linden's sprawling
In the presence of those above
With family and friends enthralling.

There, lovely lawns lay open
Like our eagerly joining hearts;
On the hush, enduring words are spoken
As our journey together starts.

Know, I will meet you there, always
In those timeless and loving places
Until the tracks of all our days
Lie etched upon our smiling faces.

So, as I take your waiting hand,
Gently . . . and quiver at the thrill,
I promise my Love will faithfully stand
Like the grand, old tree at Poplar Hill.

My Better Half

Shall I compose for you flowery words
To boost your self-esteem
Or build some treasure conceived
In the night's grandest dream?

Perhaps, I could obtain for you wisdom
So all would think you to be most wise,
Maybe, affect your heart with some potion
I could so easily devise.

I could bring you gifts, until
You were overwhelmed by the load
Or sweep you away to exotic places
In distant valleys or mountain road.

All given in earnest to express
The wonderful love I feel for you,
But they would be deemed to have
Arrived too late, be too little and too few.

For, God Himself, I know, did bless you
Abundantly from the beginning because
Each day you bestow such goodness even
Poor losers, like me, believe they're winning.

To Mother

Mother's Day comes once a year
But her children's day is always here;
A call to this one, dinner for the other
Countless blessings from a loving mother.
She has, in labor, brought us all to life,
Shared our laughter, stood by us in strife.
Who could fully acknowledge love such as this
With a card, a plant or Mother's Day kiss?

Sound Familiar?

I'm a man of charity and
A model of self restraint;
In today's world, a rarity,
Against me not a single complaint!
Did I mention my mental clarity?
A snoop and a meddler, I ain't!
I'm also immensely fair, you see;
You know, I might be a saint!
If you detect an air of conceit,
It's a minor flaw for such a heart
And don't take offense when I repeat
The details of everything I start.
You know, I'm the one to beat!
I've got the horse before the cart.
Why shouldn't I have the best seat
Given all the good I impart!

A Dream?

As I slept,
Wrapped in the nights quiet and peaceful sounds,
    A sleek red fox appeared,
Running before a pack of baying hounds.
    At first, with little or no effort,
He eluded their every advance . . .
    His fleet footed agility,
Afforded the hounds virtually no chance.
    It seemed that the fox
Ran long into that now restless night,
    Until just before dawn
He stumbled, exhausted from the endless flight.
    The crafty red fox
That had once tipped before the chasing hounds,
    Now ran frantic at their noses,
Just ahead of the relentless pursuit sounds.
    Then finally, with every ounce
Of his stamina completely drained,
    Only to face the gnashing hounds
And hunters with their clubs remained.
    So then it was, that I
In startled unconsciousness was awoken
    To ponder this dream
And of what significance it had spoken.
    But the rooster crowed,
Breakfast was made, and dawn on time arrived,
    To bring the news
That, 'the Prince of Life', my Father, had died.
    As I started to grieve
And tears began to blur my downcast eyes,
    I realized, my Father, honoring me
In life and death, had come to say his good-byes.

Ebba Tin Win

"Would you like some fish this lovely
Memorial Day morning, Ebba Tin Win?"
"Why yes! My husband and son find
Them quite delightful now and again."
"They're cleaned and chilled, ready to cook.
I'll go and fetch them from my boat."

As I returned, this gift firmly in hand
I remembered those noble men who had
Given their lives for the freedom in this land;.
Their absence a trusted companion of mine.
So, I brought the fish in their names,
A secret token of their sacrifice, to devote.

For a moment, we stood at the garden
Under the eaves of her front porch
While she explained to me chocolate mint.
Then, seizing the light of that eternal torch
She offered, "I use it to make a delightful tea
And for you, I have some in store!"

So, I took the chocolate, mint tea
Of Ebba Tin Win and all the liberty
That those brave men could not provide
For themselves and hoped that they would
See good deeds being done in America, ...
In their names . . . . Forevermore.

The Writer's Seminar

I've met many-a-man under the sail
Whose salacious rant, swearing and blither
I'd rather hear than that of Kait Gale
I swear she'd make a flower wither.

Her cohort became less than humanity,
An object of her scathing derision
And I, cringing at her profanity,
Questioned my own literary vision.

I'm sure her poems might be quite good
Had I bothered to seek them out.
But, her personality gave me no wood,
What could the rest be all about?

There's something familiar in this paradox;
A simile that I should know. Yes!
It's like not opening a wrapped-up box
Because of the big, ugly-assed bow!

You see, I could be like her and the rest
Of those purveyors of crass and crude
But, I carry it proudly under my vest
To shelter the yet, untainted multitude.

Spirit Acknowledged

I know You're there, never far away
From the snow-white cloud's silver lining,
And likewise when skies are gray
And the sun refrains from shining.

From above the grand old trees
Your comforting Spirit calls to me,
Whether over the rustling of leaves
Or birds singing ever so sweetly.

There's nothing I face alone
For You, my Lord, are always there
To ease whatever I should bemoan
My life's burdens You always share!

Catbirds

I watched the catbirds come and go
In their coal black caps and slate
Feather show. Their distinct songs
Filled the trees and places on the ground
Where I saw flickers of gray
And heard their faint rustling sound.
They did not leave like the end-note
Of the boisterous jay.
Rather, it was some time before I
Noticed the catbirds had faded away.
I can only speculate as to the
Scene of their demise,. but, I guess
Their heads are with the chipmunks;
Another house cats grizzly prize.

Only Words?

In an utterance from my breath
That no other soul could hear
I implored, "forgive me Lord,
Your Wrath upon me I fear"!

Without hesitation, He sent my
Way the much needed release,
Restored my heart's delicate harmony,
My mind's coveted peace . . .

As usual, I acknowledged His Mercy,
Gave thanks for the healing gift
And marveled how, without consequence,
The veil of darkness He would lift.

Then, casually I looked up, my
Gaze settling upon my victim's eyes.
There my careless words were etched,
Embedded beyond the day he dies.

Oh . . . There is no way to take back
The words given an approving nod,
'For man shall not live by bread alone
But by every Word from the Mouth of God'!

Two Faces of Cats

I love my little kitty
With her sleek mottled fur.
I like when she sits on my.
Lap to kneed and softly purr.
She also prances outside
With her tail high in the air,
Face-rubs the corner post,
Then fixes her hunting stare.

With programmed intent, she
Crouches low to stalk her prey,
My woodland friend, the
Chipmunk, will surely die today.
Without remorse, she drops his
Limp body squarely on my mat,
Then turns to her food dish . . .
I really do hate my cat.

The Gift

Though garland and wreathes
Sparkle to my delight,
'Tis the Star of Bethlehem that
Occupies my solstice sight

Even the vermillion and white
Of Santa, I know well
But the swathing clothed Babe in
The manger symbolize my Noel.

Nice are the wrapped surprises
Tucked under the decorated tree-
Wonderful is the gift of Christ Jesus
And His Love for me!

My Answer

After the spat, I sighed, "What's great about today?"
And the answer came, "My daughter is here,
There's nothing more or greater to say."

Then, I asked, "What shall I do tomorrow?"
Again, an answer came, "Love my daughter
And kiss away all of her pain and sorrow.

For to secure her life and place upon the earth
Has been my goal and my passion
From time primordial, ignited at my birth.

Oh!, she is fair like the twinkle of a morning star,
Or the bird songs at dawn awakening life.
In fact, she's the essence of all that we are.

So, ask me not again, 'What shall I ponder or do?'
For that which is cherished upon all the earth
Is walking in the care and company of you".

Tears

Oh, precious flows of water,
Your presence is too kind.
From within me you well;
My waiting eyes you find.
A tiny drop appears at first
A sparkling gem upon my lid
The start of rivers eager to burst
Releasing emotions I hid!

Sunset at Currituck

As the sun laid its orange face, softly
On the horizon's waiting shoulder,
Clouds ablaze in light-on-blue
Cast an amber glow on every
Little field stone and boulder!
And when I thought You could
Thrill and impress me no more,
A skein of silent geese took command
Of the western sky and the full
Moon rose on the opposite shore . . .
And so it is, My God, that I, in awe,
Praise Thee today! For Thy, Glorious Majesty
On the Earth is the light upon my way.

Because I Am

Where ever I fish,
God always accompanies me there.
    His presence transforms the day
Into a heavenly affair.
    I've never seen Him
In His plain, every day clothes
    Since He's worn something unique
To every place I chose!
    Today, His robe is adorned
With ominous, dark-cloud-beasts
    Charging in with tamed,
White maned lions from the west.
    His sash is a brilliant rainbow,
Quietly forming in the east
    Under the blue sky
And golden light from His Royal crest.
    I usually thank Him
For making such a spectacular show
    And bow my head
Or tip my hat before I smile and go.
    But He knows my Love
For Him runs far deeper than praise
    Because each day I rise
To show it in a thousand other ways!

Paradise

"Today, you will be with Me in Paradise!"
Were the words of the Lord to the thief,
As they hung together and paid the price:
One impaled for the mere taking
The Other simply for His belief.

These words are so misunderstood!
They're the cornerstone of man's creation;
The expression of eternal brotherhood
Not a pardon or to bestow
Some last minute bit of elation.

Had any of his followers
stayed with him, been there until
the bitter end, Our Lord would
have been defended by them
instead of his new found friend.

So, I recall the Master's Love
Each morning, noon and night
And pray to Our God above
To live uninfluenced and unaltered
By the greed of men or their might.

Smithover

Views of ancient mountains gracing summer air,
Morning mists lying on the river Greenbriar, so fair,
Forests bathed in the bright sunshine of the day,
A place in the heavens for a word to say . . . .
Nothing contrived or imagined from afar
Simply, events stated just as they are.
Grassy hillsides sloping gently to inviting ponds
Filled with catfish, bass and wild iris fronds,
Humming birds sipping from golden cups of primrose,
Wild turkeys sharing the ripe blackberries . . . I froze
To watch two spotted chestnut fawns
Scamper across those West Virginia lawns.
Old fences weathered gray rising from the sage,
Bright yellow flowers nestled in my journal's last page
My only burdens . . . . fishing tackle
And another day added to my age.

Thanksgiving

I was there when the earth passed by the sun
A rock come-to-life to be with God as One!
And though I'm thankful for every pleasant circumstance,
How can any be greater than life itself, perchance?

A Birthday Prayer

Lord, You alone have set upon us the seasons
And sent the rain that makes the flowers grow.
And though, I'm sure You have Your reasons,
I wonder why some are fast, others quite slow?
While, I realize, this and all the rest
Are really none of my business or concern,
I'd like to make just one small request . . . .
Please, keep on Your schedule my birthday's return!

A Few Small Details

Some days I feel the sweat,
even experience the pain
    And see my arms
out-stretched to the nails; restrained.
    Yet, there's no blood on my face
from the woven crown
    And no sacrifice in place
to claim the renown.
    So, then, I must acknowledge
the duality of my belief;
    While, I aspire to be the Lord,
in reality, I'm the humble thief.

Commitments

Where are the Essenes?
I cannot find the 'Sons of Light.'
Likewise, the Shakers, it seems,
Have withdrawn from sight.
And where is the Holy Spirit
You so perfectly instilled in me?
Am I also without lasting merit?
Perhaps, I never knew Francis of Assisi!

The Search

Like Jesus and his disciples,
I spent the night beneath the stars
On the fallen needles of a White pine tree.
Without a blanket or coat,
Just the moon's warm light. .
An apple for breakfast
Was all that stayed to comfort me.

So, when the morning sun rose
Over the distant hill,
I broke the three day fast
And drank the juice of the pome
And there I sat without pomp
In the summer morning chill
Waiting to rise and walk
The garden path to my home.

I wished my Lord had come there,
To rest not far away
With the other young men of His choice,
Whom I also Love
But the whip-poor-will
Was my companion to wait for day
And the new light brought
Only the mourning dove!

Nimbacova

Alas', we are here in our sanctum
Where the deer are at ease and play
And we, like they, escape the thorns
That gentle Nimbacova casts away.

Far from life's pesky little scorns,
We gather at the river and strife disappears
Whether we shake and shiver
Or bask in the sears of the mid-day sun.

It's here, we always start the process
Of the heart's unwinding, in rain or shine,
Without string or twine,
It's our family ties we're binding.

Some days, we hunker down with a book
Or gather 'round the table and listen
To stories a twistin' the truth a bit
For smile or a certain look that's been missing.

It's a chance to recall those special places
Like under the waterfall for mid-day baths,
Hitting tennis balls or along the paths . . .
It fills our hearts with refreshing graces.

There's humming bird fights on the wing,
Boards that creak, cows that mooo . . . too.
The squeak of the swing, and you, Yes you!
At Nimbacova, there's peace in everything!

At day's end, to the porch, we retire
And anticipate the whip-poor-will,
Who'll sing above the night time choir
When the days fun turns to evening still!

As colorful moths fly and water shoes dry,
We recount the wonderful Cowpasture days
And make plans for upcoming demands
That will, again, take us our separate ways.

Then, we watch intently as the moon rises
And lament leaving too soon on the morrow.
Amid stars falling and echoes of the past calling,
Again, sweet Nimbacova's peace, we borrow.

The Acknowledgment

I never met another man
Under the Black Cherry tree
    Or shook another juice-stained hand
That had picked and eaten recently.
    So, as I ate and pondered
How it must have been and
    Glimpsed the quiet peace
Of our Father's eternal garden,
    He acknowledged the same
And offered respectfully,
    "There are not many, my son, given
The choice, that stayed so close to Me."
    Do not stand in awe
Because of an encounter such as this,
    His presence is available to all
Who seek His Righteousness
    At the table He sets for you and me
Under the fruiting Black Cherry tree.

Author, Antrim Coast of Northern Ireland, 1973

SECTION III

The Inheritance

My beloved mountain, where have you gone?
Blanketed in haze far after dawn.
Your summit hidden and form scarcely there,
Where is your image, you so generously share?

Introduction

From my Journal, June 1st, 2004

Two Days in June

'As I began the assent up the great Blue Ridge from the foot hills of Central Virginia, it had long been apparent that this was an exceptional day! The air was so clean and fresh that every tree's leaves shimmered in the cool, sunlit mountain air. However, the full impact of the day's brightness and clarity overwhelmed me as I looked out across Albemarle and Nelson Counties, onto a valley of green forests and fields. Every feature of every mountain was distinct; every ridge, hollow and glade, every leaf, tree and blade of grass shined bright, What Majesty! What a sight!

The longer I stayed and the more I saw, the greater I realized the awe of what was spread out before me. As I viewed His Creation, without distortion, I imagined that God must have some pride at having achieved such a wondrous thing as the Earth, It was then, that I felt it . . . . I became enamored with the Spirit of the Lord.'

June 2nd

'Today is essentially the same, as there is not sufficient alteration of the air mass to change the exceptional clarity of the day. My step-daughter had also acknowledged its rarity, so we went to Elk Horn Lake in an effort to take full advantage of its inspiring beauty.'

June 3rd

'*I* re-ascended the great Blue Ridge, this time from the west, as I returned home from the Shenandoah Valley. I could already see that the distant mountains were again cloaked in hazy, gray ozone and the near mountains were returning to their familiar, dull gray-green. As the continuous stream of automobiles whined and roared behind me, I realized that out of the last 365 days, the fossil fuel that runs them and a host of other technological advances, had over whelmed and altered all but two. I also knew that the sparking creation of the Lord was still before me . . . That His pride and its potential transfer to my spirit remained. It was just much harder to see, much, much harder for me to feel and I lamented the loss . . .'!

Before the clean air act of 1990, the mountains of central Virginia were completely obscured on many summer days. Since then, the air has gotten significantly cleaner but according to the National Park Service, the Shenandoah National Park and the Blue Ridge Parkway still have the poorest air quality of all the parks throughout the country. Most days, there is still some distortion because of excessive ozone in the atmosphere and on many days the mountains and foot hills appear as gray humped dinosaurs, visible in form but not in detail. A few times each year, they still disappear completely. Because of the guide lines set forth by the Clean Air Act, each year the air quality has gradually improved so that today "blue bird days" are once again fairly common in central Virginia. Now, in 2012, there is talk of relaxing these standards because, according to some, the cost of maintaining clean air through government regulations is "reducing industry profits" and "causing economic problems". I can only respond to such selfish desires with the words of my Lord who said "what profit a man if he should gain the whole world but lose his soul."

Air quality is only one of the many natural systems being altered by the unrestricted and careless activity of man. Such ultimately life changing dynamics as habitat loss, invasive species, over harvest of wildlife populations, and the dispersion of toxic substances to mention only a very few localized problems are having an ongoing and cumulative effect on the systems that man ultimately depends on for his well-being.

We are on the verge of allowing our almost total focus and dependence on the condition of the world economy, to permanently alter many of the natural systems that underpin life on the earth. Please, note that I am *not* referring to debatable scientific studies or political propaganda used to facilitate resources exploitation or protection but rather to personal observations from years of striving to learn and understand how the existing ecosystems can support human life. Specifically, my own! We are fast approaching a time when every person will have to acknowledge not only the beauty of the earth and its life but also the importance of preserving the stability of its systems. In short, everyone will have to make some personal commitments to its preservation or resolve ourselves to allowing its loss.

Every day I lament,
Distraught at what I see . . .
Obscured mountains, clouded waters
And tainted humanity . . .

So, I started a war
The first battle waged within . . .
Purging my heart, re-directing my life . . .
Vowing to start again.

Hearty Souls

I awoke one day to find some hearty souls
Of the earth nestled against my foundation.
Not dependent upon me for their survival
But rather, to guard against their annihilation!
For, there are those who cannot see the earth or its
Life, from atop the mound of their exploitation.
And others, who see it clearly in their own back yard
But ignore their impacts on other lands and nations!

Words from Afar

Do not misunderstand me!
I'm not chastising only you.
It's the unrelenting activity
Of us all that will destroy man
Upon the earth before we're through.
It will not be by the resolution
Of the One or the restraint of another
That the repentance will be achieved
But by the immersion of us all, just as it
Was proclaimed, by those who first believed.

Views From The Skyline

From the Big Meadow, I viewed thee,
Knee deep in the blue berries' mountain glade.
At your sight, I succumbed to the memory
Of the clean rocky waters I used to wade.
Vividly, I came to recall the clear reflections
Rippled so slightly by the wind
And longed for thy watery perfections.
How long must I dream and pretend?
For, I really could not see thee at all;
The valley is obscured by ashen, ozone haze . .
Thank God, my mind is clear this fall,
For the Shenandoah looks like honey-mustard
ham glaze!

Background Noise

I detected the clamor
From nearly a mile to the north
And watched the sky
In anticipation as they came forth.

They were tiny spots
Near the bottom of the lowest cloud
In formation, the five flew south,
Precisely south, fast and loud.

Alone, I stood, my neck stretched
To watch the cranes fly by.
Above two thousand feet they flew,
No other birds drew nigh.

From where I watched,
No one else acknowledged the flight
Until I showed another young man,
Who marveled at the sight.

So, much is happening above
Our heads and under our noses
That's hard to witness
Or appreciate from this bed of roses.

The Inheritance

I weep for you my son and daughter!
For, I am here, you are there.
Would that I had fought harder
To overcome the Laissez-faire.

My strength and I are now retired.
You, must rise to the occasion;
Change the hearts of an uninspired
And wasteful consumer nation.

You have expressed grave concern!
Unfortunately, it's not misplaced.
I would have used less in my turn,
Had I known what you would face.

I leave you with so much undone;
The Chesapeake in fatal decline,
Too much heat from the sun
And the last dependencies of mine.

Then, there are the depleted oceans
Pollution laden gray skies,
Pills for every condition, and potions
To stave off your natural demise.

Don't forget, just one fish a day
Lest mercury overcome your mind.
And don't believe everything they say;
It's the economy first . . . then mankind!

I knew the right way to go
And fought for conservation.
But I required too much, you know;
Forgetting about your preservation.

Even in my miserly old age,
The opportunity was always there
To let consumerism exit the stage.
But I didn't, now I despair!

So, it is incumbent upon you
To make the inevitable adjustments.
I'm sorry there's so much to do.
And your challenges so immense!

The Ragged Mountains

That which Poe brought to mind
Shrouded in mystery and fright,
Have become, for me, hills and
Hollows of unparalleled delight.

For, to be lost in their vastness
Seems rather pleasant to me;
Then, I'd have my fill of their
Wildness and utter serenity.

Reflecting on Poe
and Others
In the Ragged Mountains

My beloved Ragged Mountains, pray
That you should be the last to fall.
Were you subject to my will, your
Lofty peaks would shoulder no burden at all.

For there is no near place where rocky
Ridges and deep fertile hollows combine
To create such a maze of forested wilderness,
A monument to Paradise sublime.!

There is such diversity of life here and
At each turn the terrain is never the same.
'There's little similarity between where you're
Going and the place from which you came.?'

So, in awe, I traversed the game trails etched
Deep into the soil of each twisted contour
Confident, through their presence I'm never lost,
Though of my bearing, I'm always somewhat unsure,

Until, on the edge of their southeast corner
At the end of a long, gently sloping arm
I emerged from the continuous, bare canopy
To view the cow fields of Poor House Farm.

In reverence, I turned toward the hollow, rising
With the stream, trickling down from the west.
For at this place, he who went before me arose.
From the din in the little farm house, he blessed.

Eighty years hence, there's nothing left here
But ashes, forlorn fences and rusted garden tools.
Yet, on the wind there's whispers reminiscent of
Laughter and a hearty "whoa" to the team of mules.

As I gazed skyward, my eyes eager to embrace
In wonder the rugged tops of the forested hills,
I was surprised to see bright shimmering
Flashes of sunlight from some objects gaudy frills.

So, in all haste, I started the accent that
Leads northwest for nearly a mile,
Wondering what object could cause such a
Blight on the mountain's stark, winter profile!

Long before I drew near the place where
I calculated the object would be,
The whine and drone of engines filled the woods
And settled, uneasily, deep inside of me!

By the time I arrived, the machines
Were quiet and sitting unattended at rest
But behind them lay a road sixty feet wide that
Stretched from the valley to the mountain's crest.

Ridge tops had been flattened to meet the
Hollows filled with rock and excavated soil.
The ground, raw and barren, was sprinkled
With its first taste of diesel fuel and motor oil!

I realized in an instant that the mountains
Had been forever altered, never to be the same
As I wondered whose strength to endure had
Faltered; what weakness had called their name?

OUT OF THE EARTH

Then, devoid of intent, my mind compared this scene
With the little homesteads of a few generations before
And my heart fought off contempt for those who, for
What need, had exploited the earth this much more.

Before I had time to answer, from that normally
Placid spirit, so deeply pierced within,
My eyes fell upon two carefully sculpted monoliths
Rising from the mountain called Bear Den.

It was the reflection of sunlight from their windows
Between stone and wood of naturally occurring hues
That interrupted my moment of quiet introspection;
My sense of order on the earth, it served to confuse.

I did not trespass further, there was nothing
Different to see, no more that I needed to confirm,
For they had cut almost every tree for the view
And planted a lawn to the barren pavements berm.

I knew that this scene repeated itself as many
Times as the monuments to extravagance rose
From the back of the mountains peak, for they
Trailed away into the distance in long, ragged rows.

I sat down that day in the leaves, my back
To the weathering roots of a blown down oak tree
And cast disparagement and curses but
Neither they nor the tears served to comfort me.

So, I arose and started back, trying not to view
The mental images of days I knew were sure to come,
When I gasped at more brightly colored ribbons
Dangling from the limbs of a sapling black gum.

Initially, I closed my eyes to block out
The source of this impending and certain pain
But my already broken heart sank anew,
As I tracked their course along the elevated terrain.

For a moment, my mind flashed to Poe and
The inspiration he obtained from this wilderness
Then, I hoped that he would never know, that
Today there's a road in and out of the "abyss".

So, I guess this marks the end . . . . this year
Of discovery in the fall leading to 2008.
The landlord here has changed and in his
Hands lies the fabled Ragged Mountains fate.

Seduction

I took my turn at the complex life
Then, shunned that persuasive wife
Who sought, with comfort, to modernize me;
To stand firm in Nature's ruggedness
And embrace the element's sweet caress;
Giving my heart to a lover's simplicity.

Man

My back is toward the woodlands.
My soul resides in them no more.
I've forsaken the trees for painted walls,
The tender grass for the polished floor.
God, Himself need not chastise with His wrath
For the Laws of Nature, alone, will write the epitaph.

Flight

Glistening airplanes streaking across the evening sky
Mark the heavens with ice-white streamers as they fly
To destinations beyond the range of trodding feet.

Some slowly fading into the horizons brilliant orange hue,
Others gaining intensity as they surge plainly into view;
Today, there's a dozen marring the winter sun's daily retreat.

My mind inquisitively scanned its vast store of information
Sorting bits of economics, physics, environment and conservation
To place perspective on this scene of humanity in route.

I imagine meetings, visits, sports, entertainment and school
A rush to utilize riveted metal, technology, and fossil fuel.
I fear I'm ignoring the obvious or leaving something out!

As the pastels of evening settled into the crisp darkness of night,
Millions of stars filled the heavens with bright twinkling light.
And the airplanes became celestial litter, blinking without end

In that moment their relevance became as clear as the winter sky.
They're the ultimate symbol of disregard, the quintessential fly by!
A wasteful, fleeting, winged distraction I simply cannot defend.

O Whale

A whale has cried, A whale has died
And lies motionless upon the surface of the sea.
Two tons of blubber and sixty barrels of oil
Is all's to show for a whale and twenty men's toil.
Now, upon the shore those salty men sit
Spinning yarns of 'Dar she blows' and another hit.
And the days pass to seasons and on to years;
Another generation is watching, hoping to see a whale
But, there's only the sea mingled with men's tears.

Celebration

A new land's been found across the sea
It's shores washed by two oceans;
It's hills made just for the free . .
A place for all of man's silly notions.

It all started out so good
Each thing well-based and unsoiled
But everyone did as he would
So that in Freedom all was spoiled.

Each new idea came to be fulfilled
Awesome things; the moon, atom and cell
Man accomplishing all that he willed.
But is it paradise or a glimpse of hell?

Spirit

I am the flowering peach,
Fragrant at the edge of the glade
And the great, towering beech
Where the turkeys came and made
A lie to scratch and dust for the day.

I live within the Red Orser
And in the waters where it stood;.
My breath's the wind that makes the forest stir
Over ladies slippers, trillium and monkshood.
Why, would we clear it all away?

Challenge

I challenge you, young American!
If, in fact, it is still so,
To rise up from your lazy ass;
Into the wilderness you must go!
Take only your eyes and ears,
Maybe, a strong looking glass,
And record what life, there, to you appears
If, in fact, there's any left to know.

Going . . . Going . . . Gone!

"You, environmentalists, are all the same"
Is what I get,
    Along with the dismissive question,
"Is the sky falling yet"?
    "No", but Ash trees in the east
Are under attack and
    Quarantines are set
To keep the Emerald Ash borer back.
    I know you scoffed
At the American chestnut blight
    And wondered what happened
To the passenger pigeon's flight?
    And still, you vehemently reject
Any evidence of global warming
    And fail to take note
Of so few honey bees swarming.
    Please, explain to me
The heart that just had to shoot a buffalo
    Or the one proud to target practice
On piping plovers flying low.
    There are no good reasons
Or justifications that would suffice!
    Sadly, without environmentalists
In the way, you'd surly do it twice.
    The Wolly Adelgid now eats
In the Hemlock's ancient stands.
    They're also going, going, gone . . .
By bug or the ax men's hands.

But you wouldn't know it,
Since you rarely enter the woods.
The mall is where everyone finds
All their "essential" goods.
Without sprays, Gypsy Moths would
Devour hardwoods in the Blue Ridge
Acid rain has killed the trout there
And nearly every hatching midge.
In spring, salamanders
Used to cross my dirt road to spawn
Now the pools are empty,
A paved highway blocks where they're drawn.
I want to cry over the plight
Of the migrating red knots
Whose epic flights are dwindling
Because of horse shoe crabs for eel pots.
"I'm just trying to make a living,"
Declares everyone who takes.
But wildlife can't support this
Standard of living, for heaven sakes!
Asiatic bitter sweet chokes my garden
While kudzu smothers my trees,
Baltic Ivy is taking over my yard
and there's honey suckle up to my knees.
If we don't stop importing these exotic
Plants, and ornamental grasses
We're going to sorely regret the day
And live forever in weeds up to our assess!

My Simple Life

Who can say lord, what tomorrow will bring
What we'll do or what new song we'll sing?
The world is so full of trade, buy and sell
The earth, mother of life, is ripped all to hell.

In summer a gray day used to be so rare
But today, we pray just for the skies to be fair.
What greater turmoil could tomorrow bring
For today, my simple life is touched by everything.

Had I known then, Lord, about global warming
Or the possibility of no honey bees swarming
My lament would have been far greater
And my protests sooner rather than this much later.

Had I sensed science would lead us to cloning and
Genetic engineering, your natural wisdom disowning
I would have fought harder, made a firmer stand
To secure my children's place, upon this, my chosen land.

Lonesome Butterfly

As a little boy, I was an explorer
Who came home just in time for bed.
Everything was something new to store
In the recesses of my empty little head.

It was not the adventures in comic books
Or complex models that interested me
But the life in swift flowing brooks
And the creatures of the woods, so free.

My friends were into the Alamo, Crockett
And everything associated with baseball;
I watched the migrating birds come and go
And collected colorful leaves in the fall.

By the time I entered high school
I was already known as the "snake man"
And spent a few days each week, as a rule,
On the creek or in the fields without a plan.

I remember summer days, then, when butterflies
Were fluttering on or near every inviting flower,
And their colorful wings formed a patchwork
Atop the milkweed, till the day's last sipping hour.

There were also armies of honey bees dangling
From the blooming tassels of tall sweet clover
And so many tending the white, Flat Dutch heads
You had to be careful what you walked over.

BUTCH HOUCHENS

On many afternoons, I would walk to the Fife's
Back yard, a rolling, twenty acre horse field,
And take note of what wild fruits were ripe
To pick and eat from their generous yield.

By then, the birds, butterflies, bees and I
Had become as one, brothers in the wild,
I saw little distinction between them,
The creatures, and me, the human child.

So, in her ways I grew up to mimic the
Otter and catch fish, except with a fly.
I learned to call turkeys with my mouth
And impressed everyone with my eagle eye.

I studied every bird, wildflower, tree,
Animal and plant, whether edible or not,
And learned their place of origin, their
Habits, and uses and none have I forgot.

I could go on for days recounting moments
And hours I've engaged nature since then.
In fact, I may know more about her than
Myself, so, I'm not sure where I should begin.

But, somewhere along the way, she and I
Changed our relationship to our detriment;
I for the peace and tranquility lost and she
For the resources and life I greedily spent.

I often search my heart for some insight
Into the reasons for her obvious decline
And the answer always comes back contrite,
"There's a correlation to the assent of mankind"

OUT OF THE EARTH

Unfortunately, not all of us agree, even
As to whether there is a natural demise,
For the friends that I knew as a boy,
React to the assertion with utter surprise!

I guess the most distressing reality,
That I am forced to reckon with in this,
Is that those young men, who usually played
On the asphalt, are now courting the mistress.

I am not one given to jealousy, so, sharing
Her many wonders I would not forestall
But I wondered about their motivation,
Commitment and love for the keeper of us all.

So, I monitored the promises, liaisons and
Engagements of some of her most ardent suitors
And found P.C.B.s, mercury, and sulfur to be
Presents of these cleverly disguised polluters.

Then, one day, I read a report that unquestionably
confirmed my greatest fear, the President
influenced government scientists to understate
environmental impact evidence every year.

It doesn't take much intelligence or attention
to what is happening today, to realize that
there's only bits of truth fronting the pack
of lies that taints everything they say.

It became painfully apparent who really
controls our lives and ultimate destiny.
It's the boys who exploit her riches
not the scientists, naturalists or me.

I realize that we all have some part in this
And would like to make amends for mine
But now, there's so much dependent upon the
extravagance, I wonder if we have enough time.

Now, when she and I meet on those sunny days
And I encounter that lonesome butterfly,
It equally grieves my heart to greet, almost
No honeybees on the sweet clover I walk by.

The Keeper

Where have the birds gone?
They're not at the feeder of late.
I sure miss their soothing song
And wonder what has sealed their fate.
Wouldn't it be tragic to discover
That something we made to disperse
Was the cause, and no other
Of their dying sealed beyond reverse!

Spirit of the Wild Speaks?

You do not know me,
For I am from a place
You have not seen.
There are no shades of gray
Or ambiguity, only black and
White . . . blue and green.

My laws are not negotiable.
They remain firm and constant
Whether acknowledged or broken,
Forever incorruptible
By power, greed, money
Or words cleverly spoken.

I am not of the concrete,
Carefully manicured lawns
Or sizzling hot streets
But of secluded game trails,
Shaded country lanes and
The sweet Earth under bare feet
.
Mine is not absolute security
Or a fortune amassed
To bankroll a lifetime
But food for the day,
The comfort of family
And sharing to the last dime.

.

You do not know me
For I dwell in places
You choose not to enter.
I rejoice in the unaltered
Body whose path is
Not far from center.

I always find potential
In human diversity and
Do not exploit the weak.
I give no advantage
For letters from universities
Or the ability to speak.

I am not impressed with
Grand towers protruding
High into the sky, for, to
Achieve and sustain such
Greatness, much is devoured
And many more must die.

Rather, I am the craftsman
Of necessity, traditional lore
And the glow of "fox fire"
Never a demander of extravagance,
Not often seeking complexity
And seldom slave to my desire.

OUT OF THE EARTH

You cannot find me for
I am in the places you
Did not think to go, in the
Simple life you didn't take
And in the self restraint
You could never show.

The short sighted look to
Distant lands to provide
For their sustenance. but,
Those with true vision realize,
That those things which are
Close at hand make more sense.

You, likewise, look to the stars for
A future home and resources to
Continue your rampant consumption.
Realizing you're destroying the
Earth but too addicted to
Comforts to feel any compunction.

Some are quick to feign righteousness
Because of the slightest adjustment
To become "environmentally green"
When, in reality, they've simply traded
One certain death for another, with
Only a few ticks of the clock in between!

You would not recognize me,
Whether I stood before you with
Open arms or tightly clinched fists.
For you rejected every alarm
And cursed the very concept of
Truth from an environmentalist.

You see, life upon the earth is a
Fragile chain linked with firm
Yet, unpredictable connections;
Once broken, un-repairable by
Meaningless speeches or
Periodic government inspections.

So, if you truly seek my
Presence, the enduring spirit
Of man upon the earth,
Look to the innocence and
Simplicity of your childhood
Before your possessions or self worth.

For, I am the one who has come,
Do not expect another and though
You do not know where I am from,
I forewarn all of the reconciliation
With Nature that awaits every
family, group, tribe and brother.

. . .Would that I were like John Muir
That my words might always endure
To remind those who enter into the wilderness
That this, of all things, contains thy holiness.

Majesty

I am upon the earth,
Having descended from the sky,
To walk this place with strength
And grace until the day I die.

I am in the heavens,
Having been raised from the earth,
To see the Glory of His Face
In this place of my birth.

For I am the blending
Of the Spirit and the flesh,
God Incarnate?—dust regenerate!
The perfect mesh . . .